MUSEUM OF LIFE

Wayne Gathers

To order additional copies of this book, contact:
Xlibris Corporation
1-888-795-4274
www.Xlibris.com
Orders@Xlibris.com

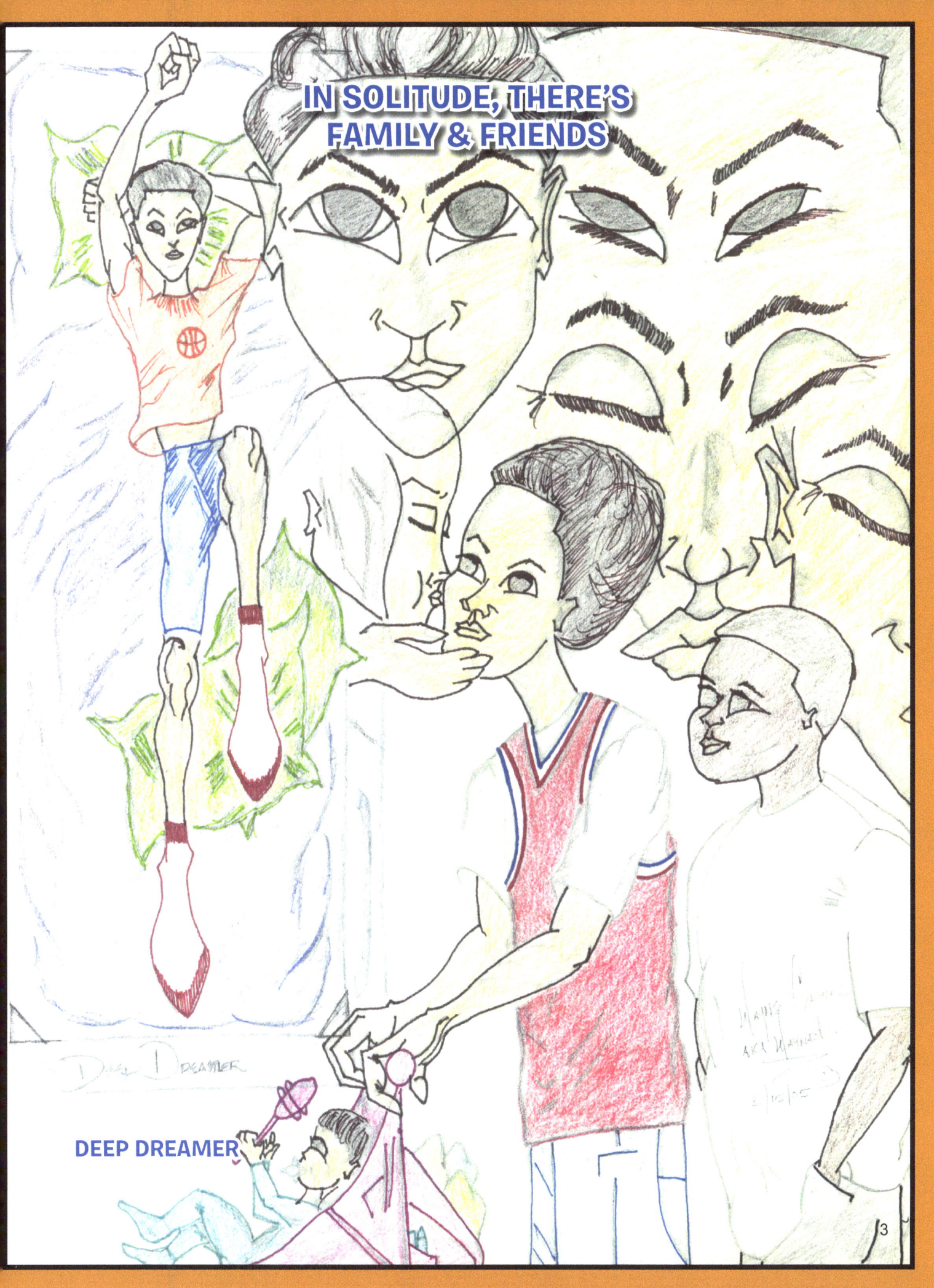

IN SOLITUDE, THERE'S
FAMILY & FRIENDS

DEEP DREAMER

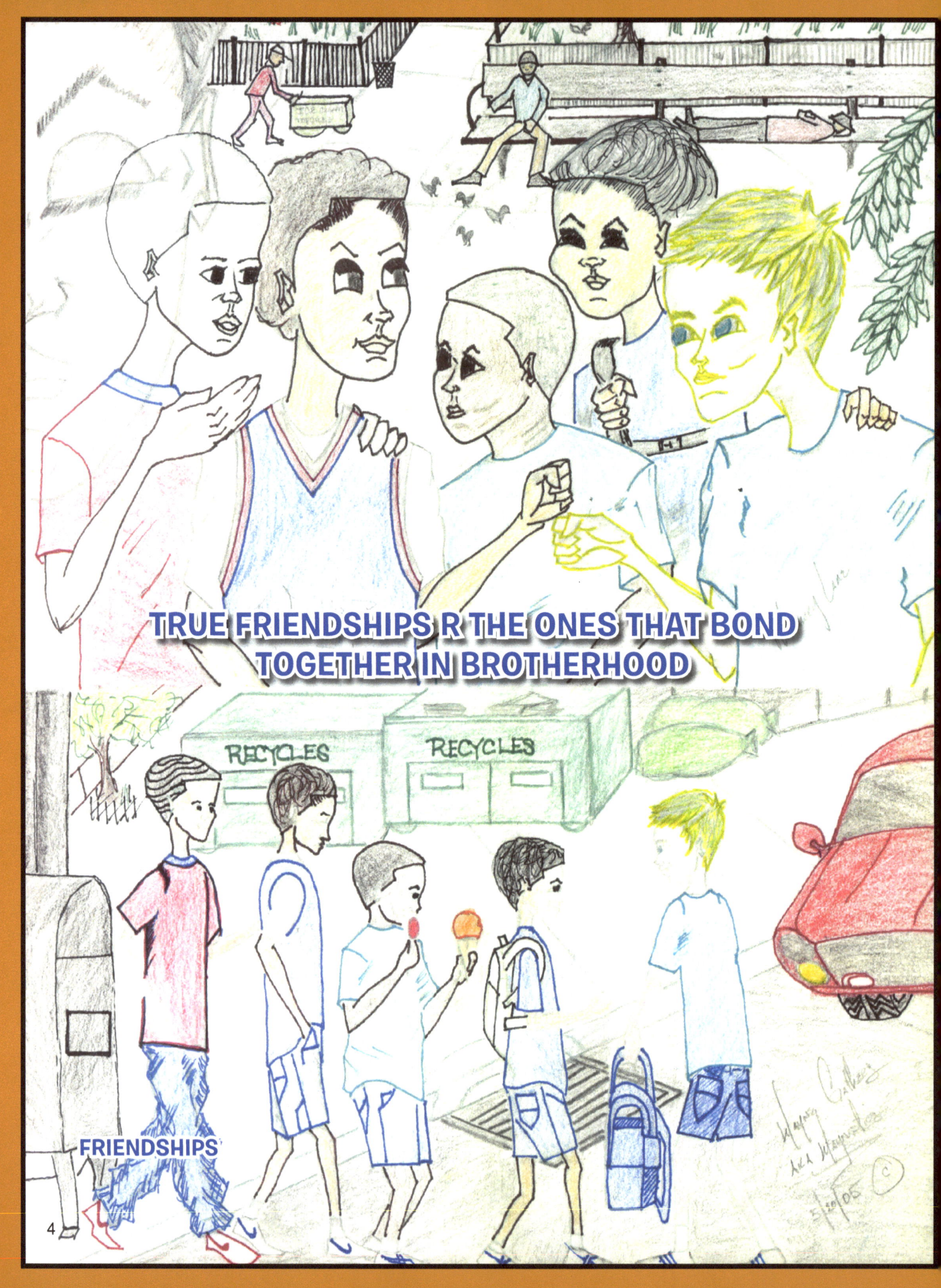

TRUE FRIENDSHIPS R THE ONES THAT BOND
TOGETHER IN BROTHERHOOD

FRIENDSHIPS

4

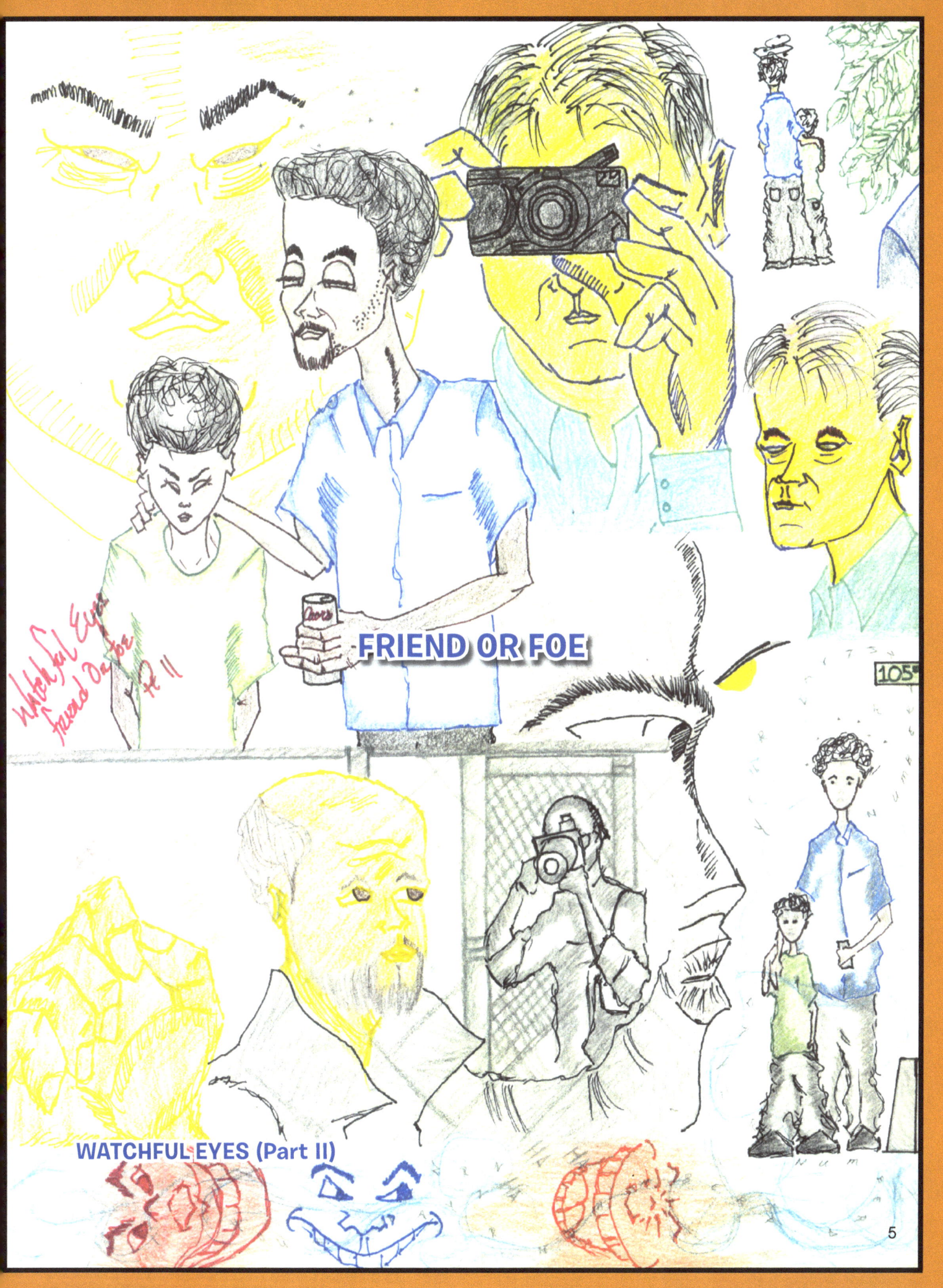

FRIEND OR FOE

WATCHFUL EYES (Part II)

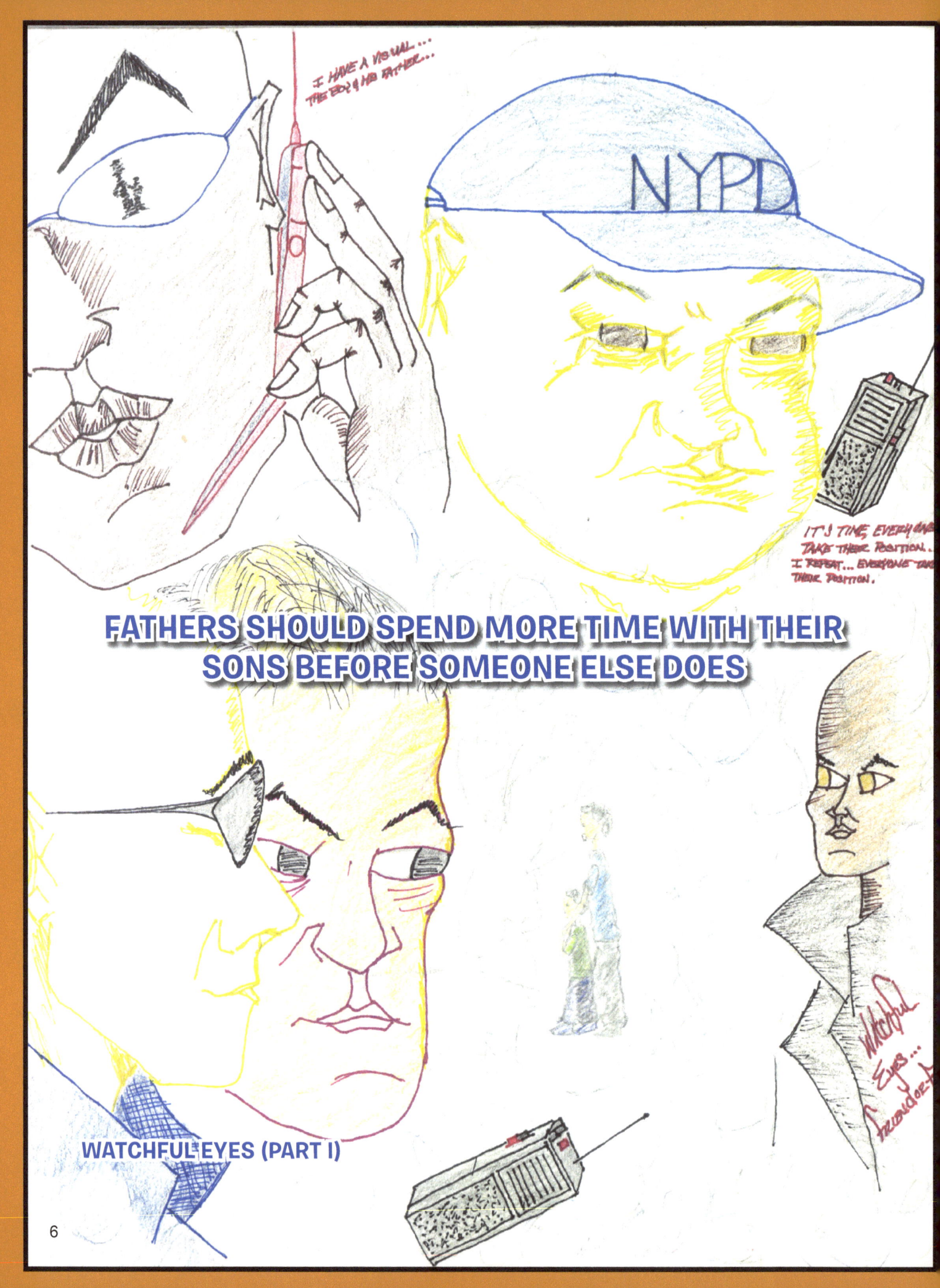

FATHERS SHOULD SPEND MORE TIME WITH THEIR SONS BEFORE SOMEONE ELSE DOES

WATCHFUL EYES (PART I)

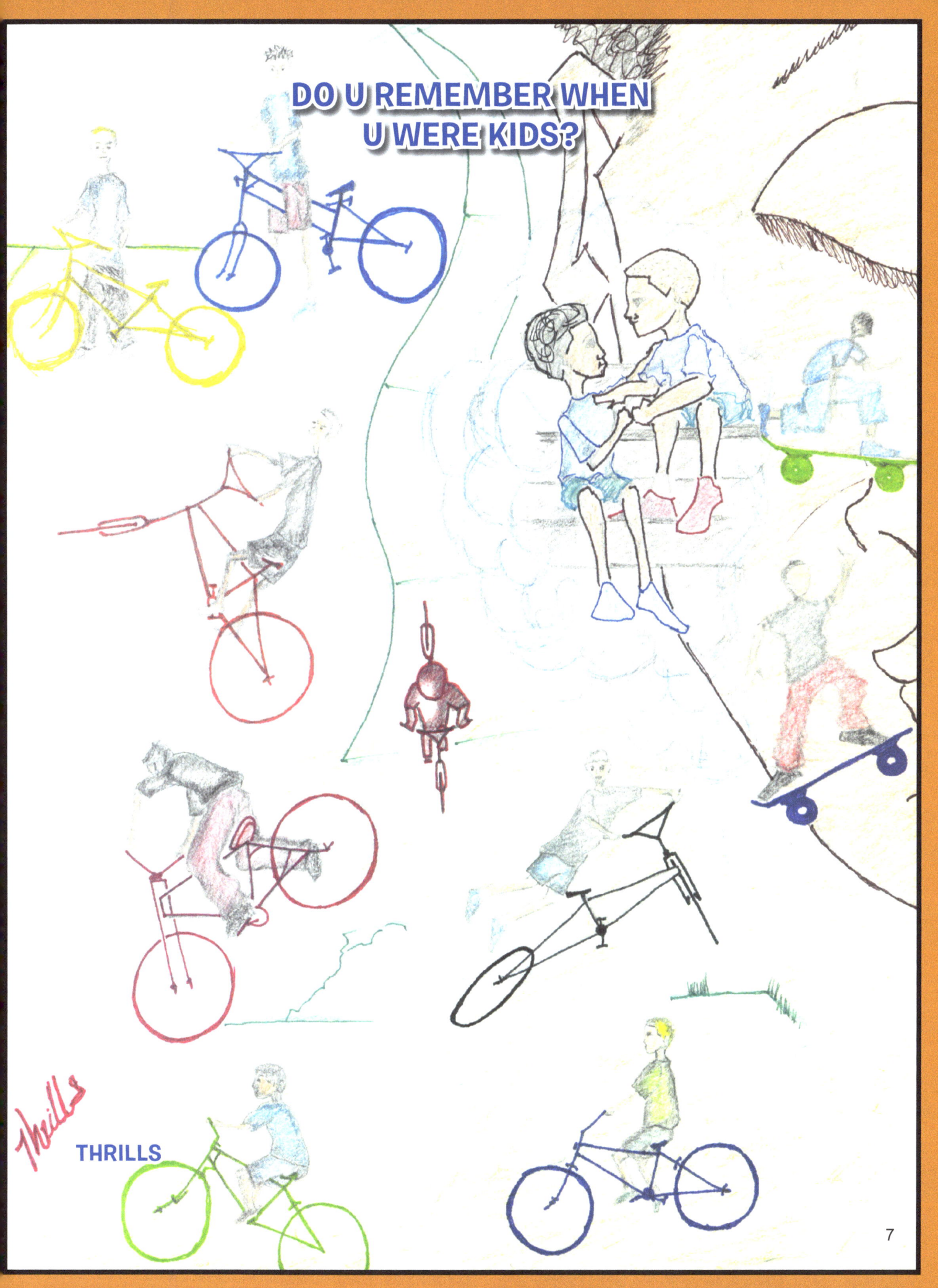

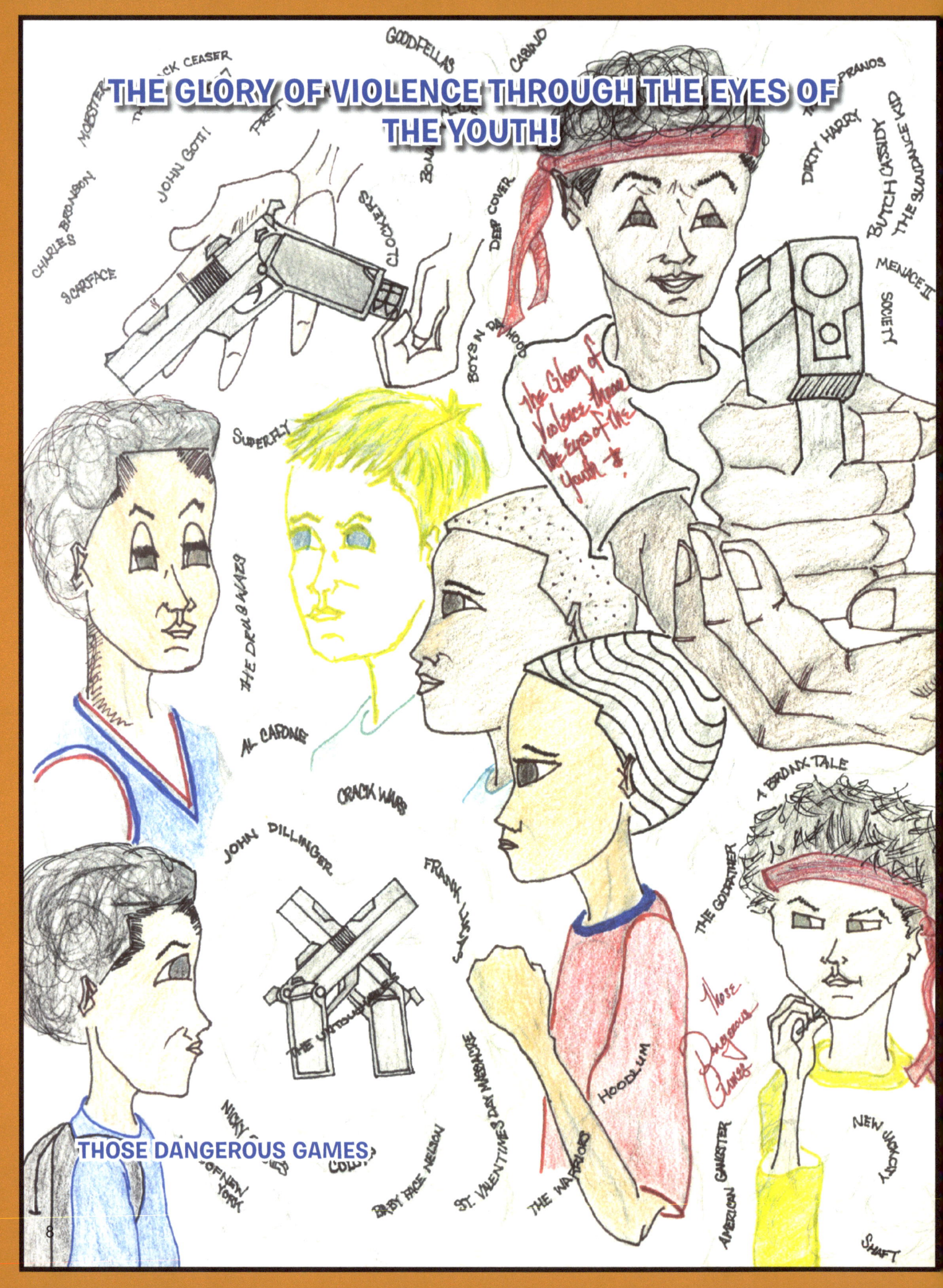

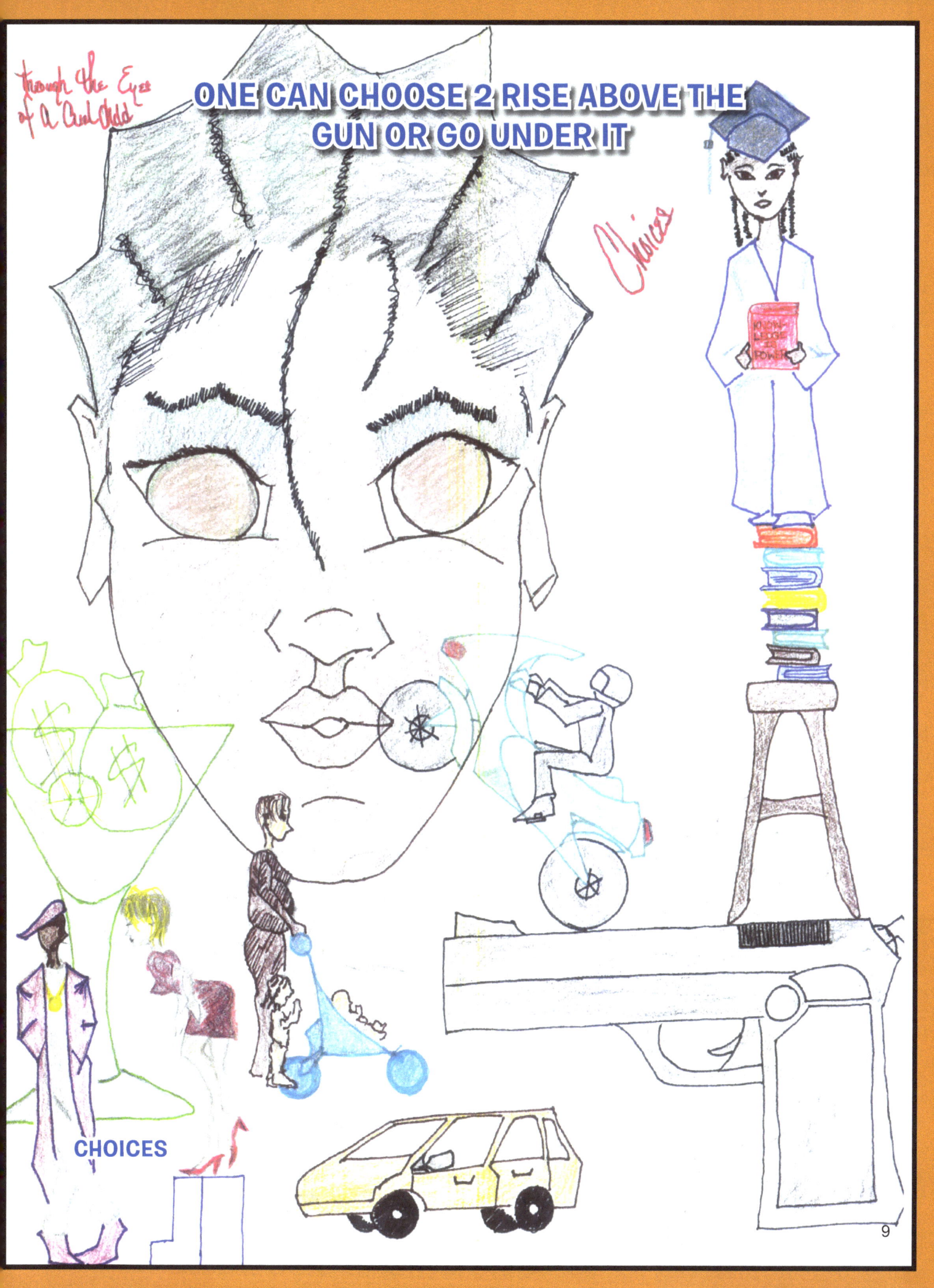

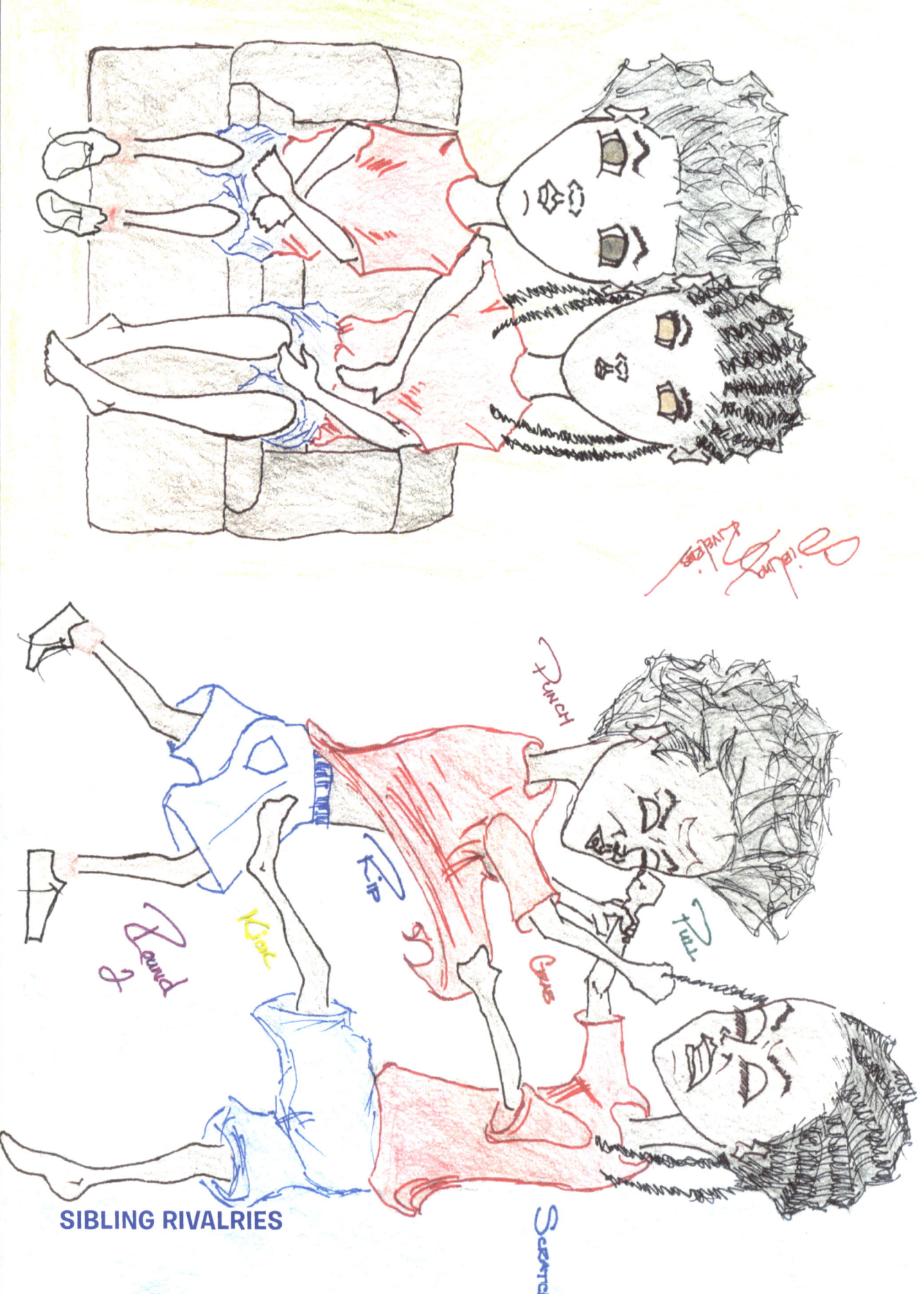

SIBLING RIVALRIES

10

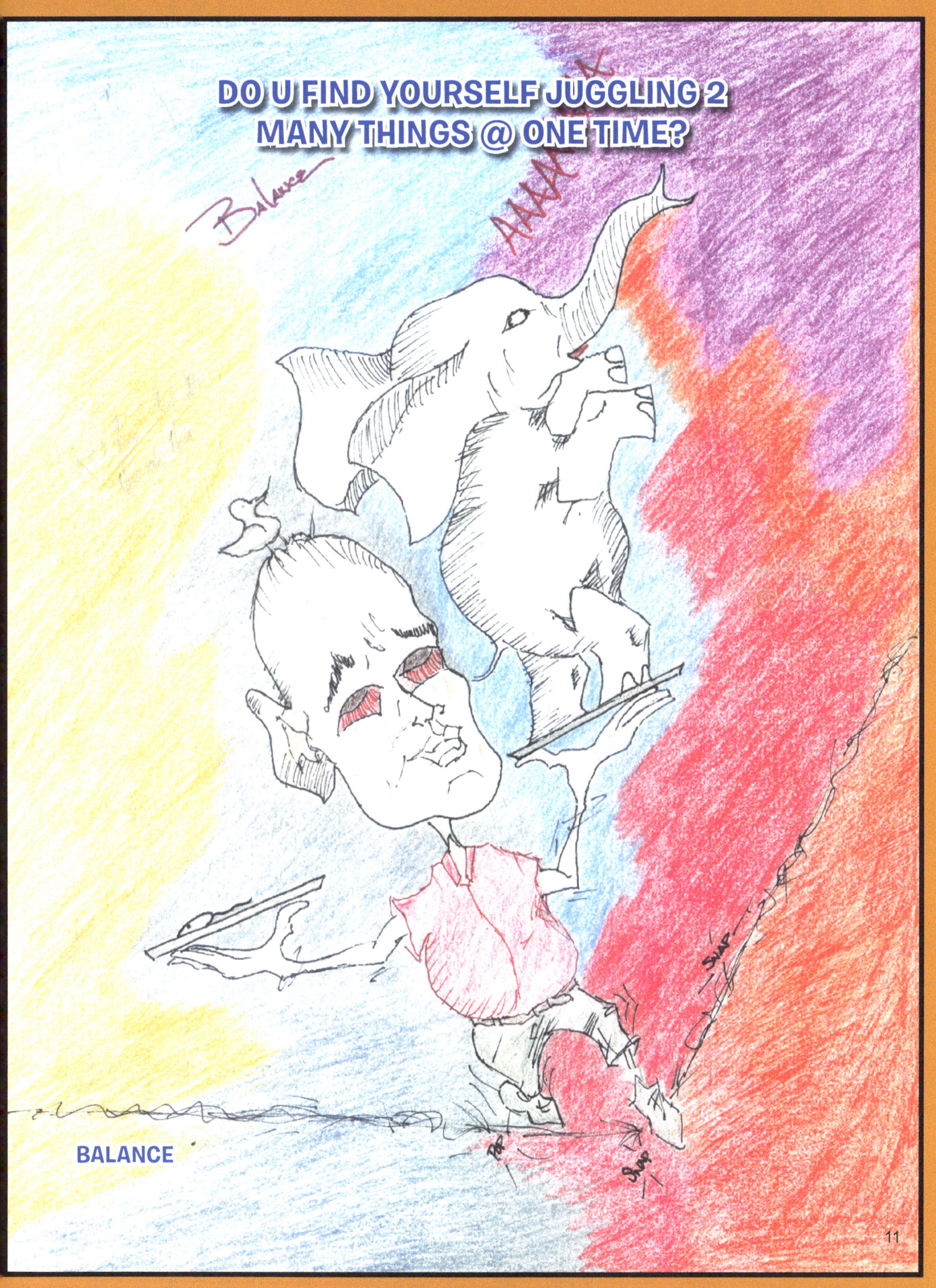

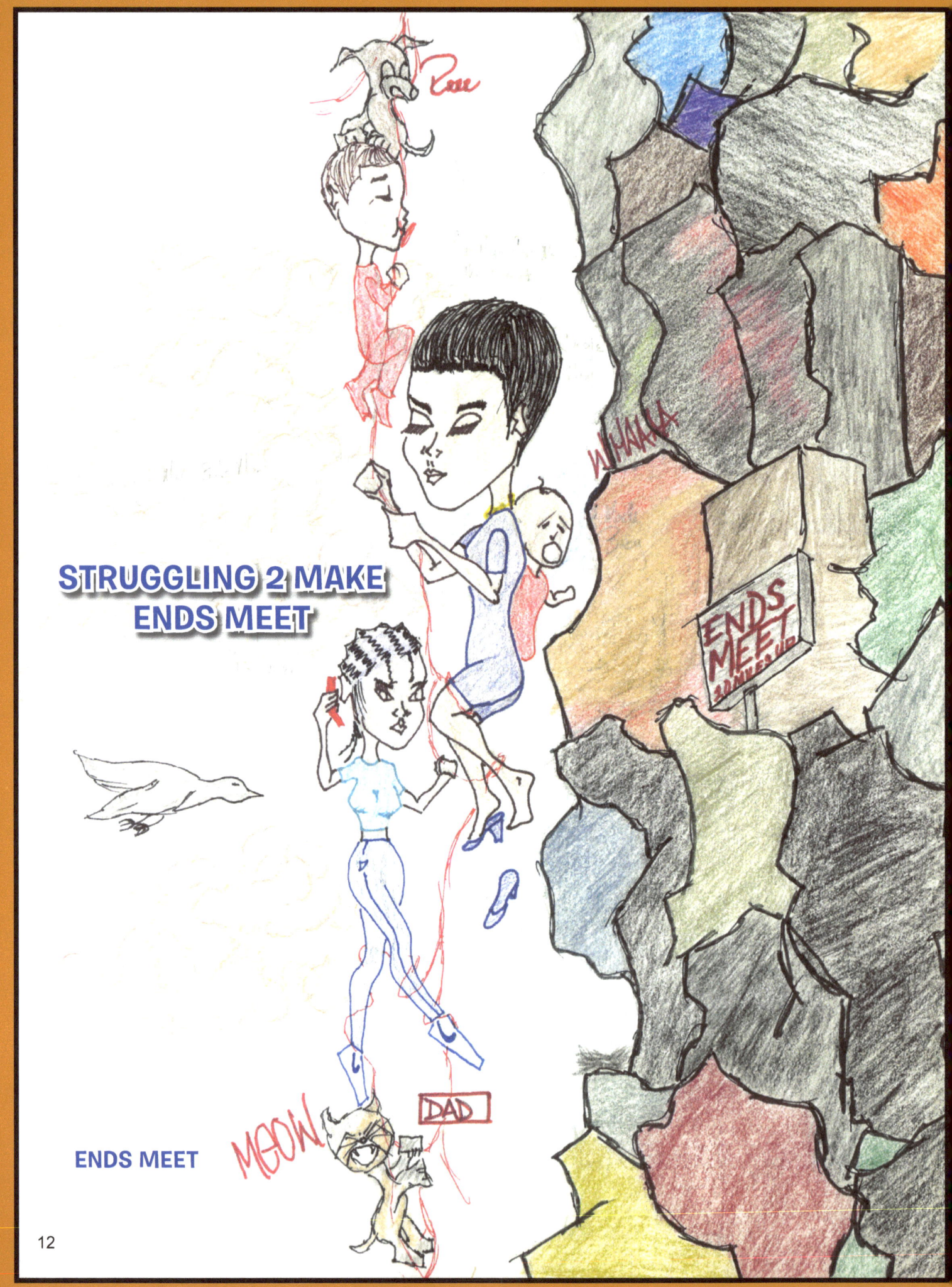

ENDS MEET

DAD, WHERE'S MOM????

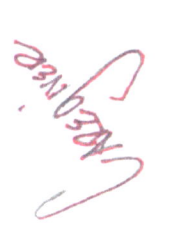

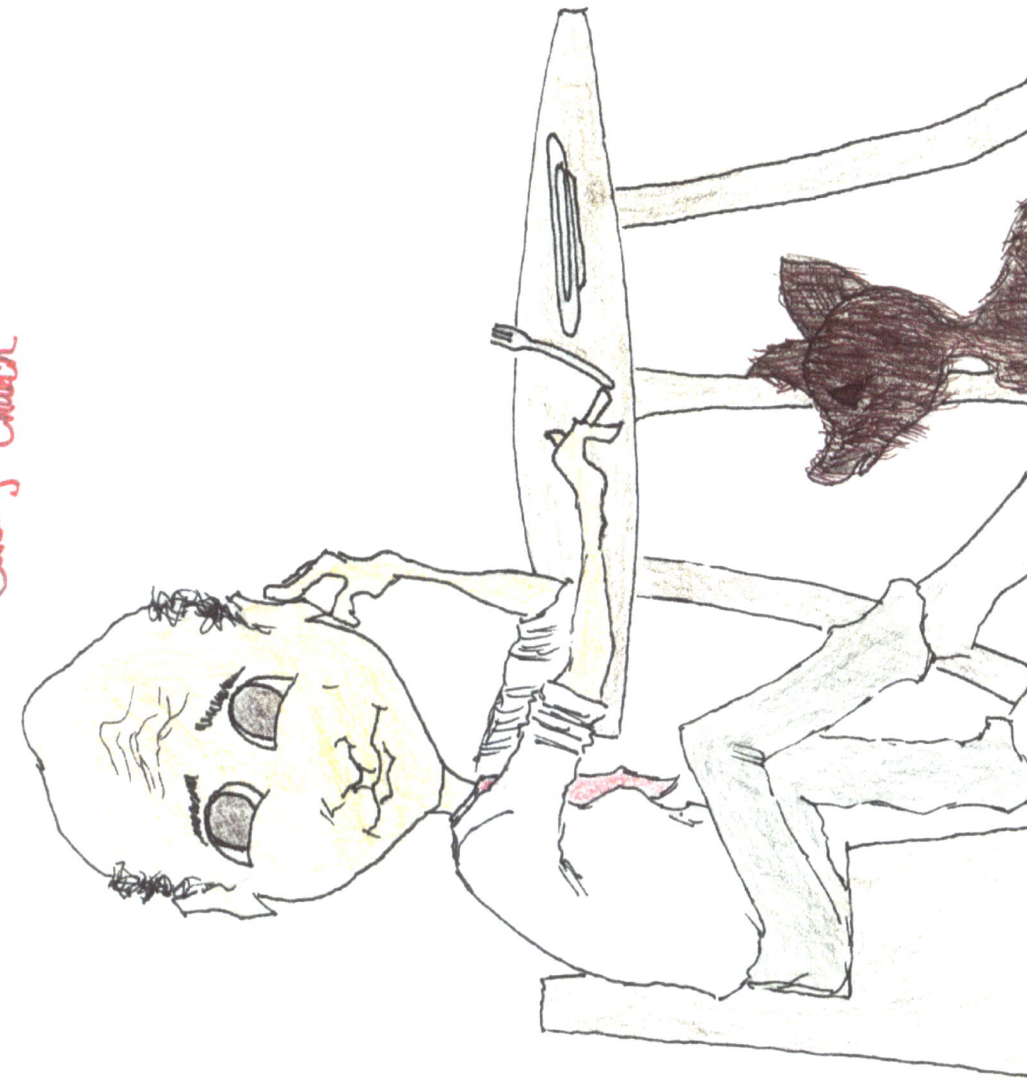

Mom's Kitchen Hours

Monday – Soup Opens
Tuesday – Not In Service
Wednesday – Vacation
Thursday – Out Shopping
Friday – Movies & Dinner
Saturday – Day off
Sunday – Church

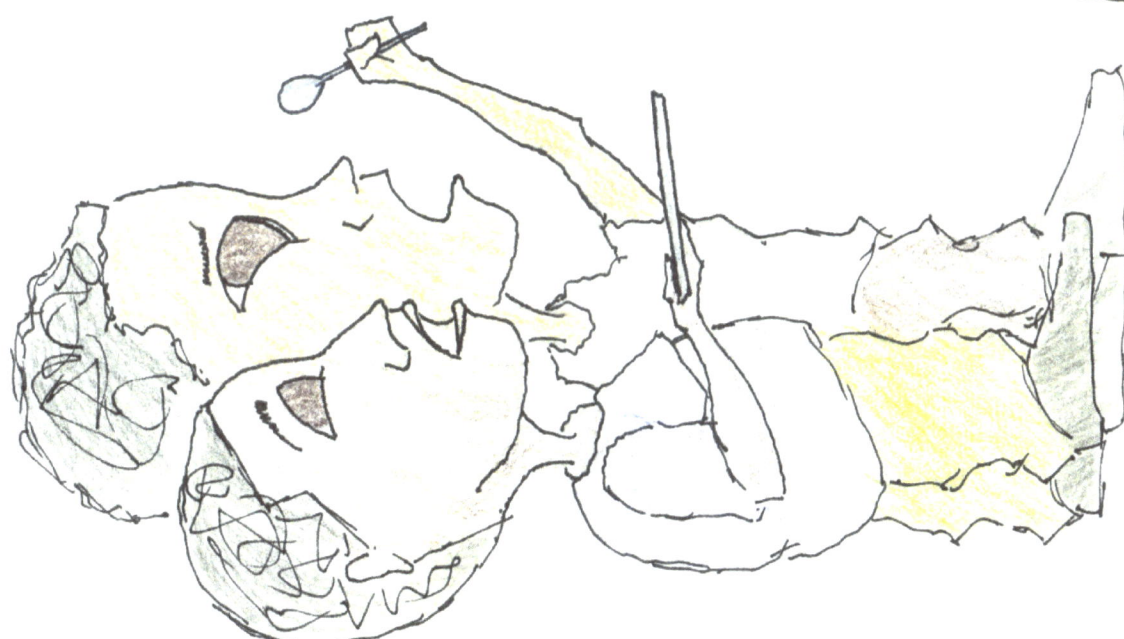

CAREGIVER

THE HAND OF MANY CHOICES

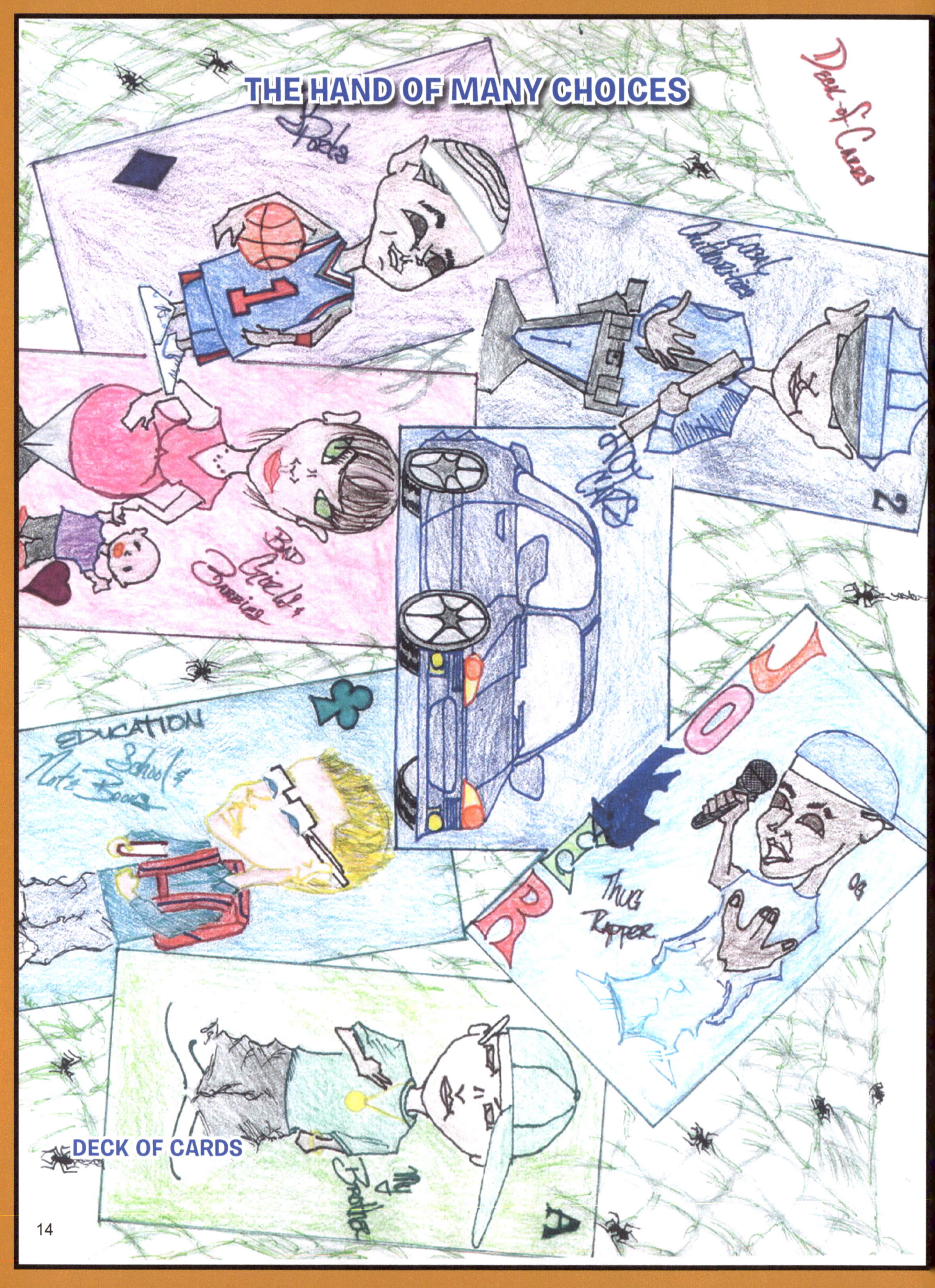

DECK OF CARDS

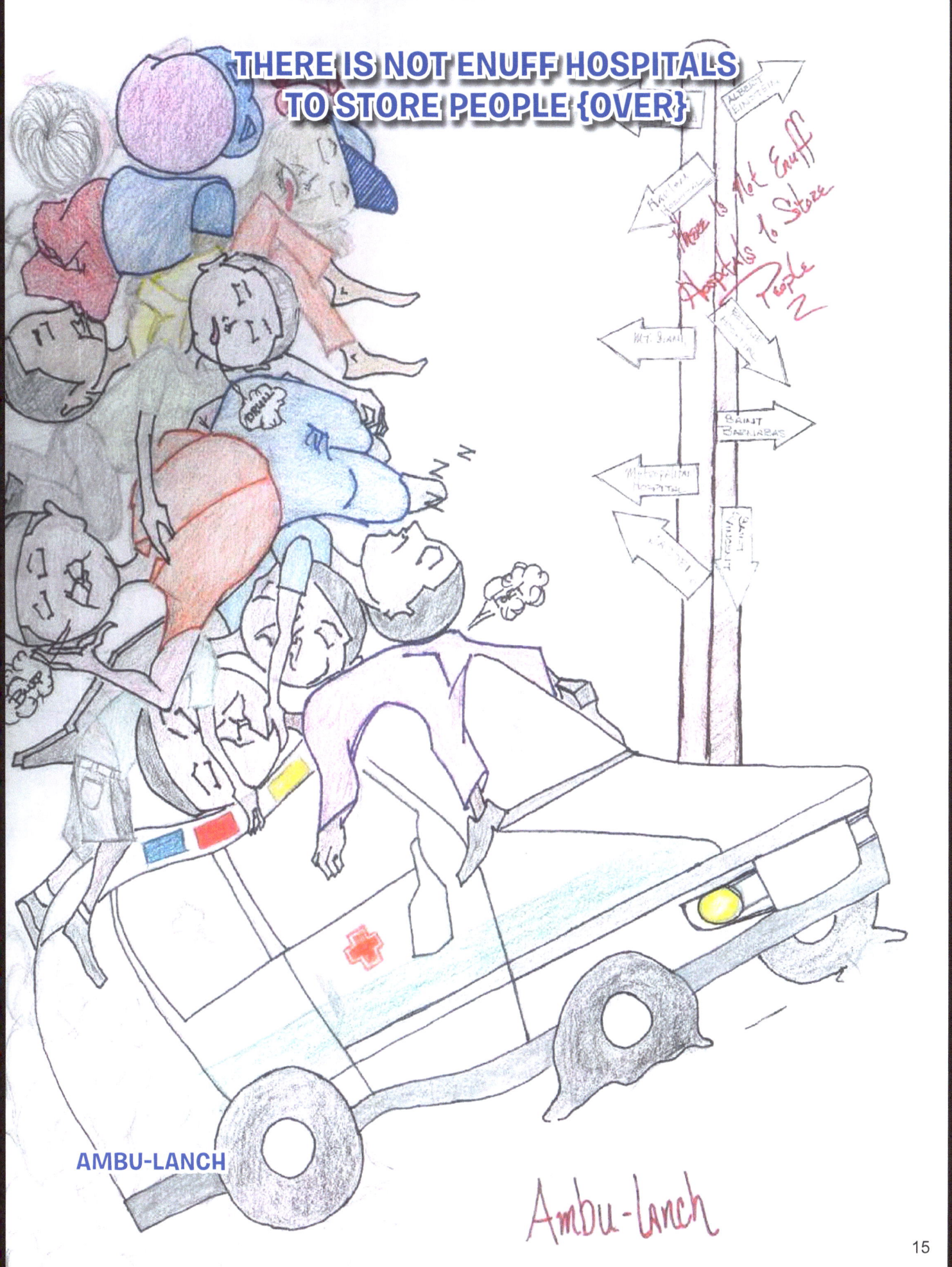

CAN U IDENTIFY YOUR SON(S)?

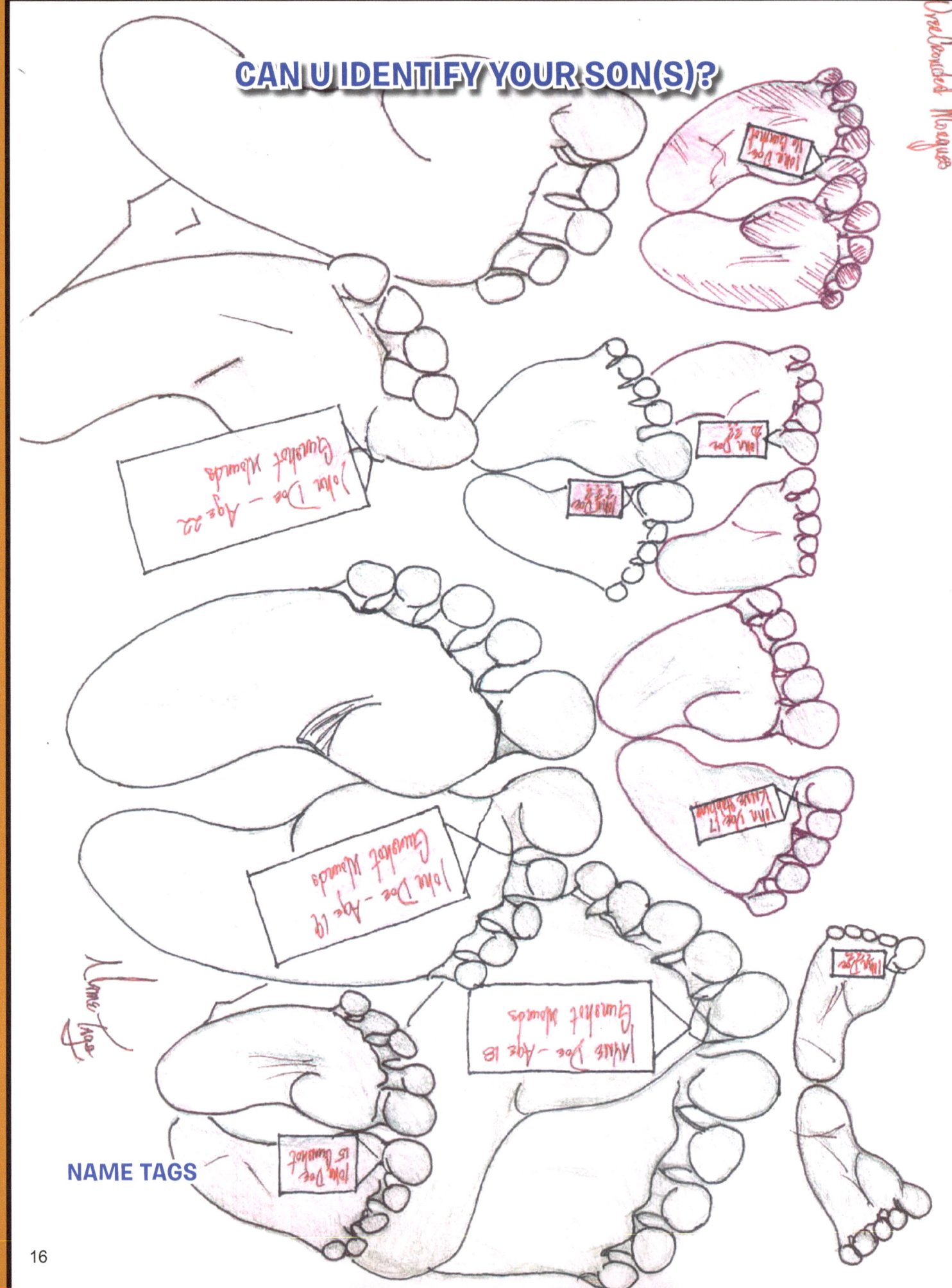

NAME TAGS

WHAT IS HAPPENING TO OUR YOUTH?

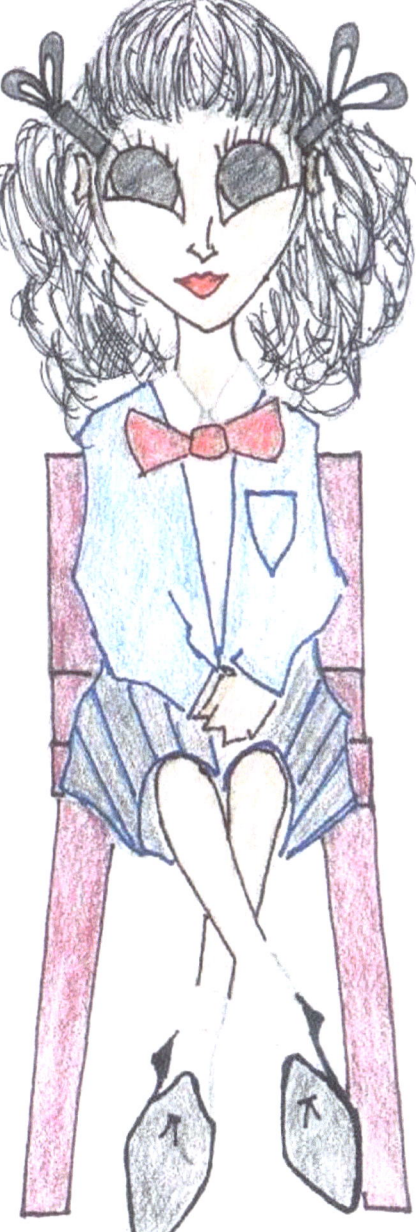

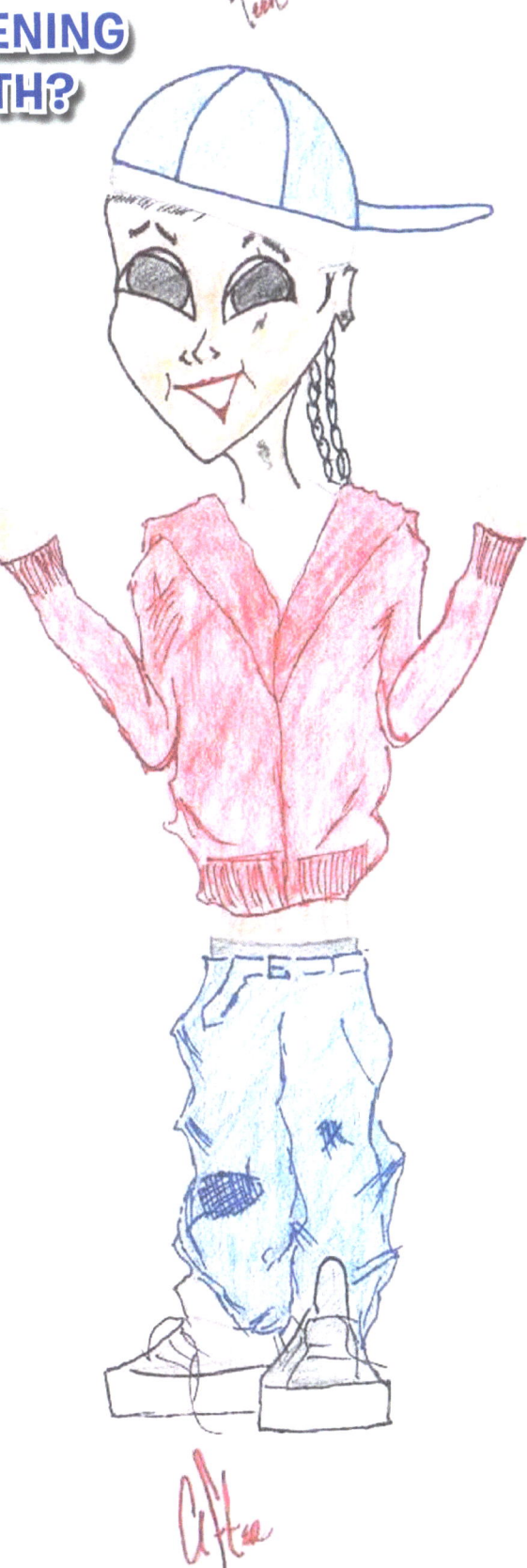

Metamorphosis

Grade School @ 9 yrs Old

High School Teen

METAMORPHOSIS

Before

- N -

After

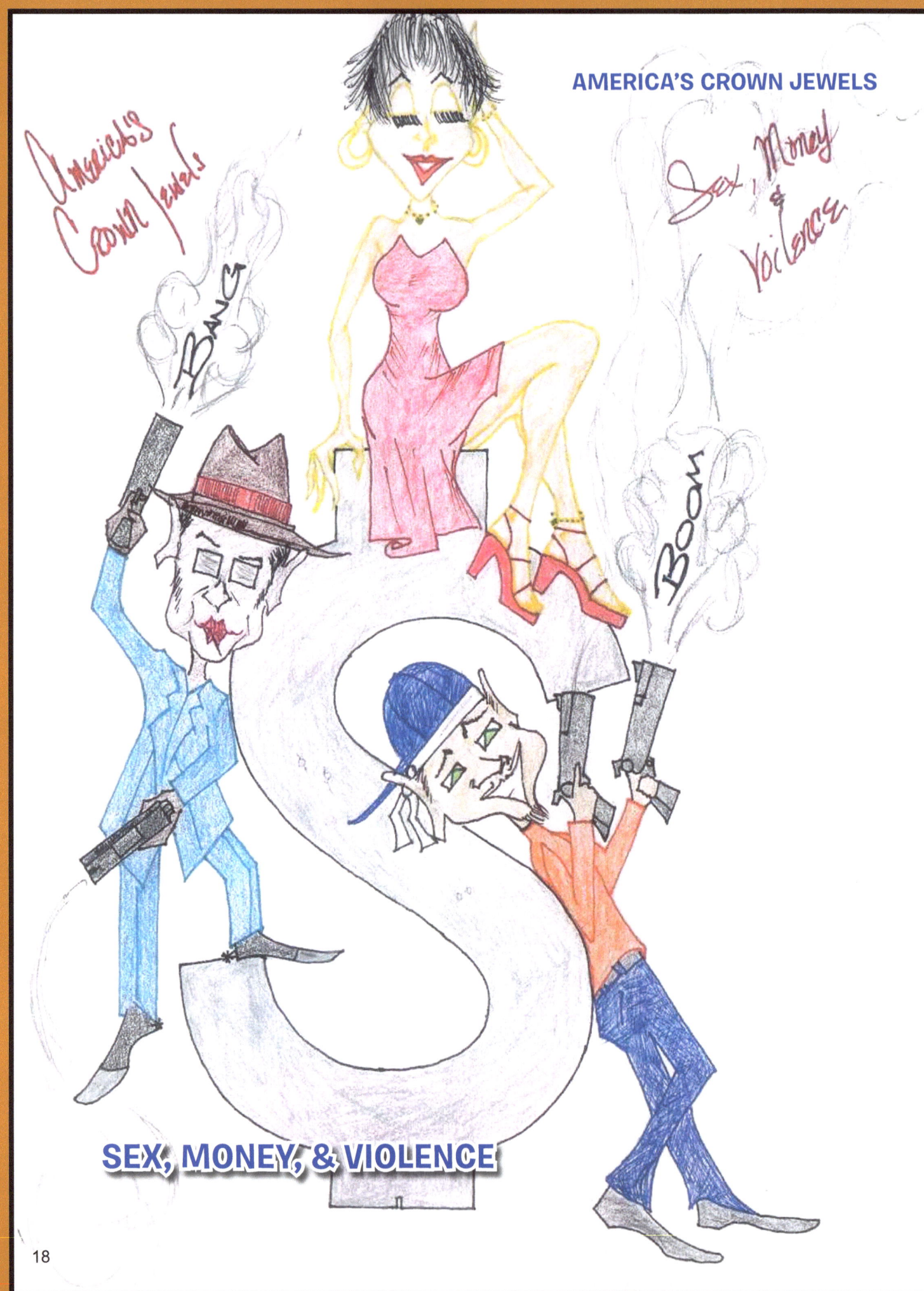

SEX, MONEY, & VIOLENCE

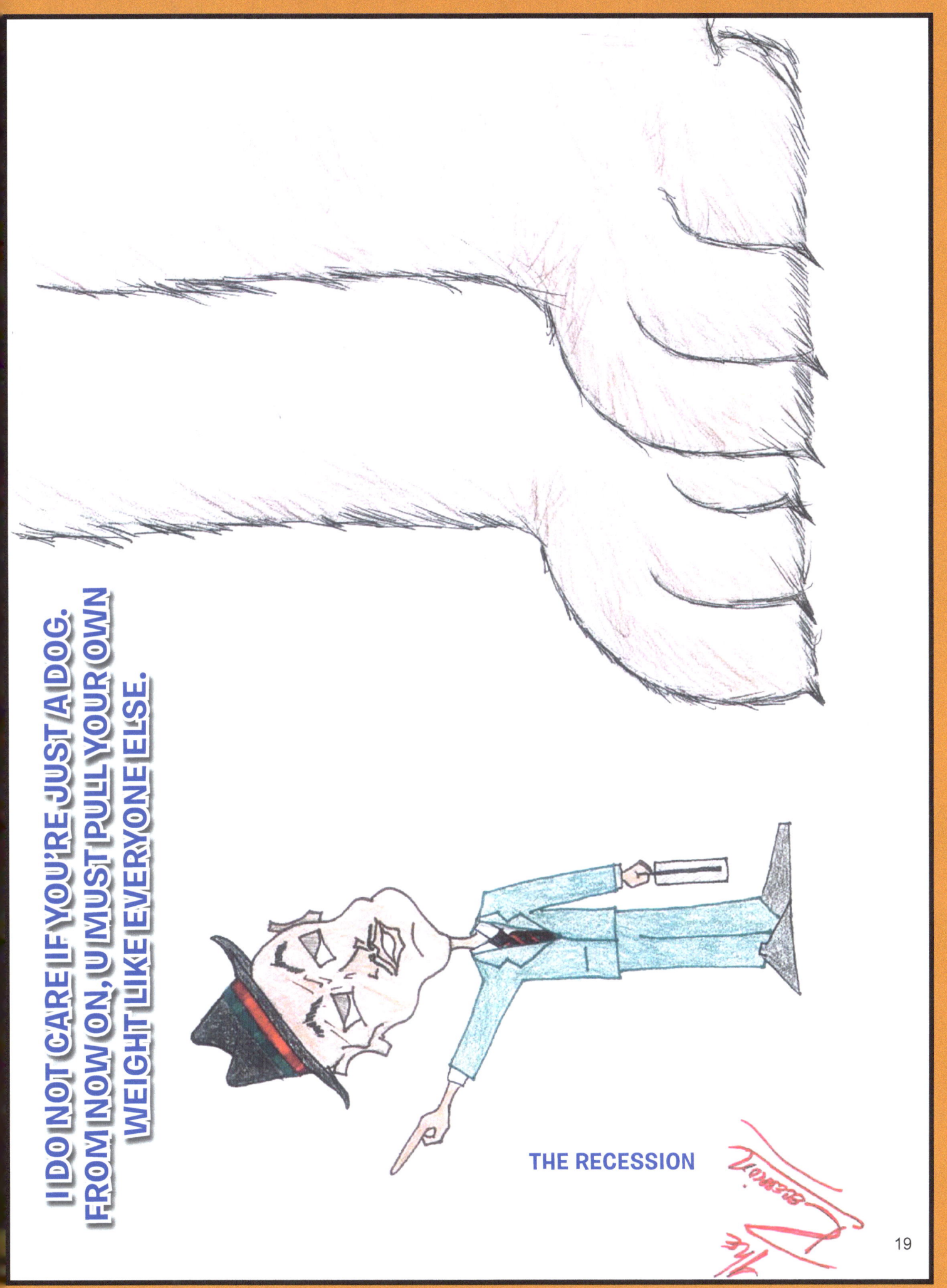

THE RECESSION

19

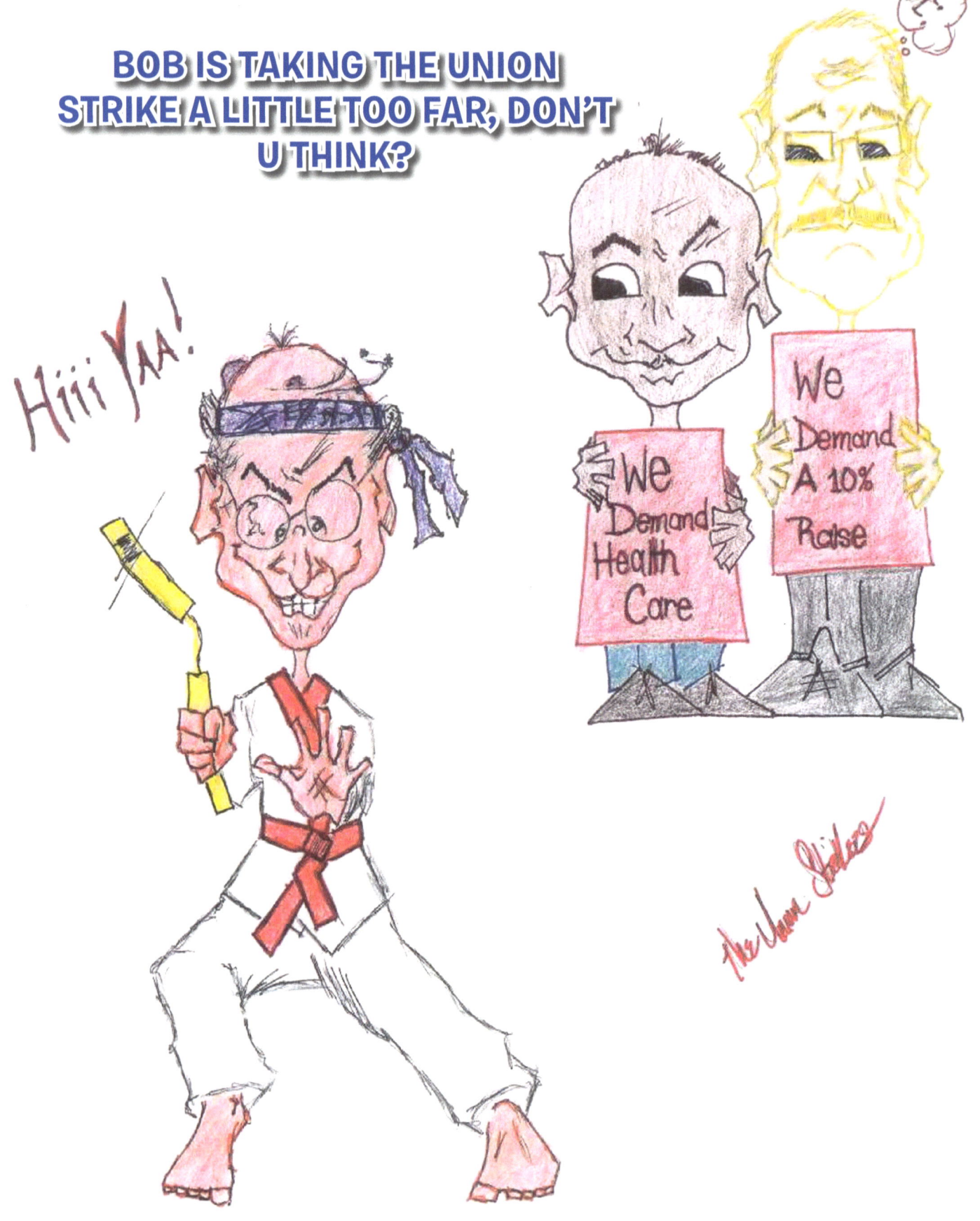

THE UNION STRIKERS

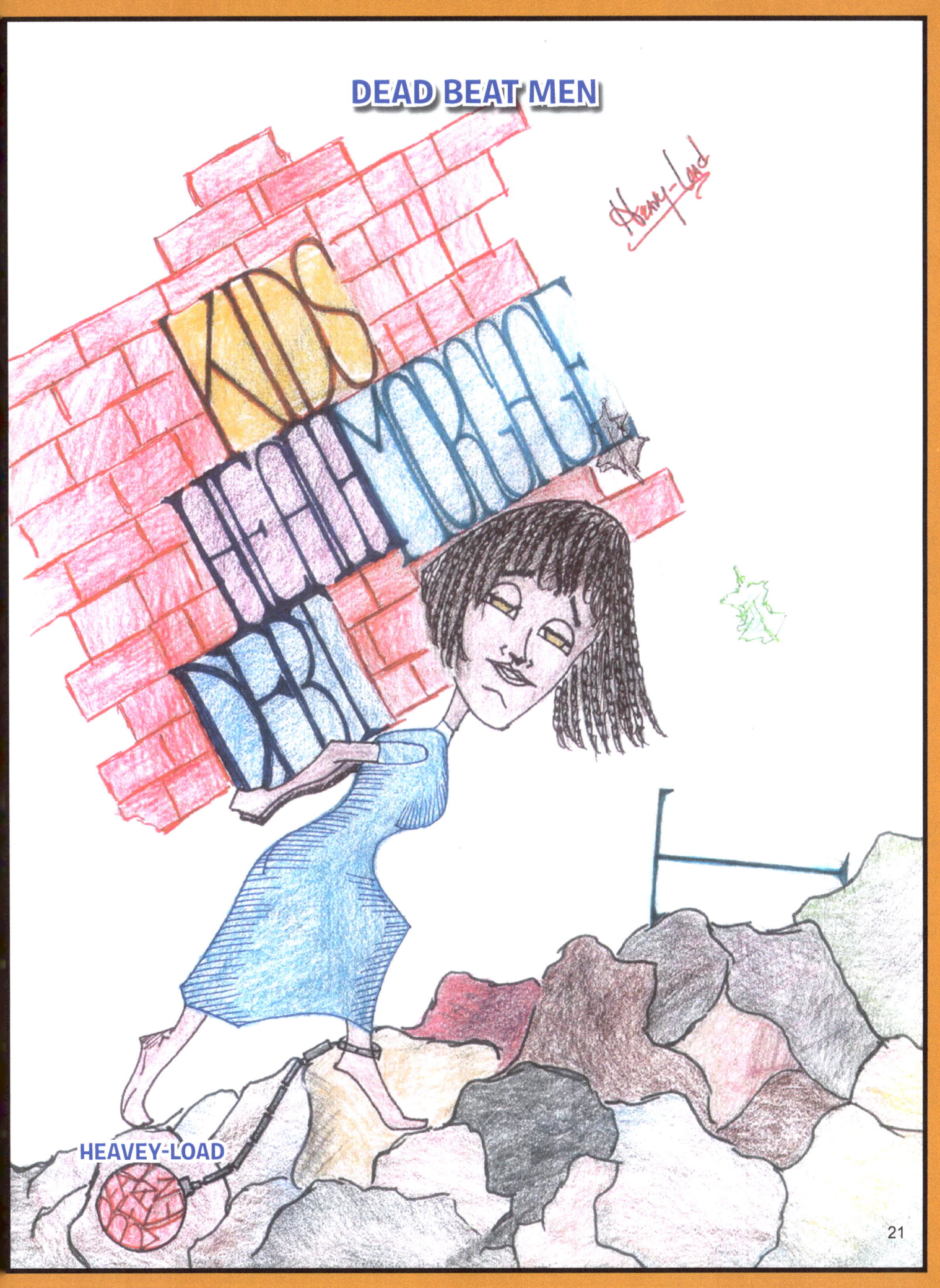

HOW MANY PROBLEMS DO U SLEEP WITH?

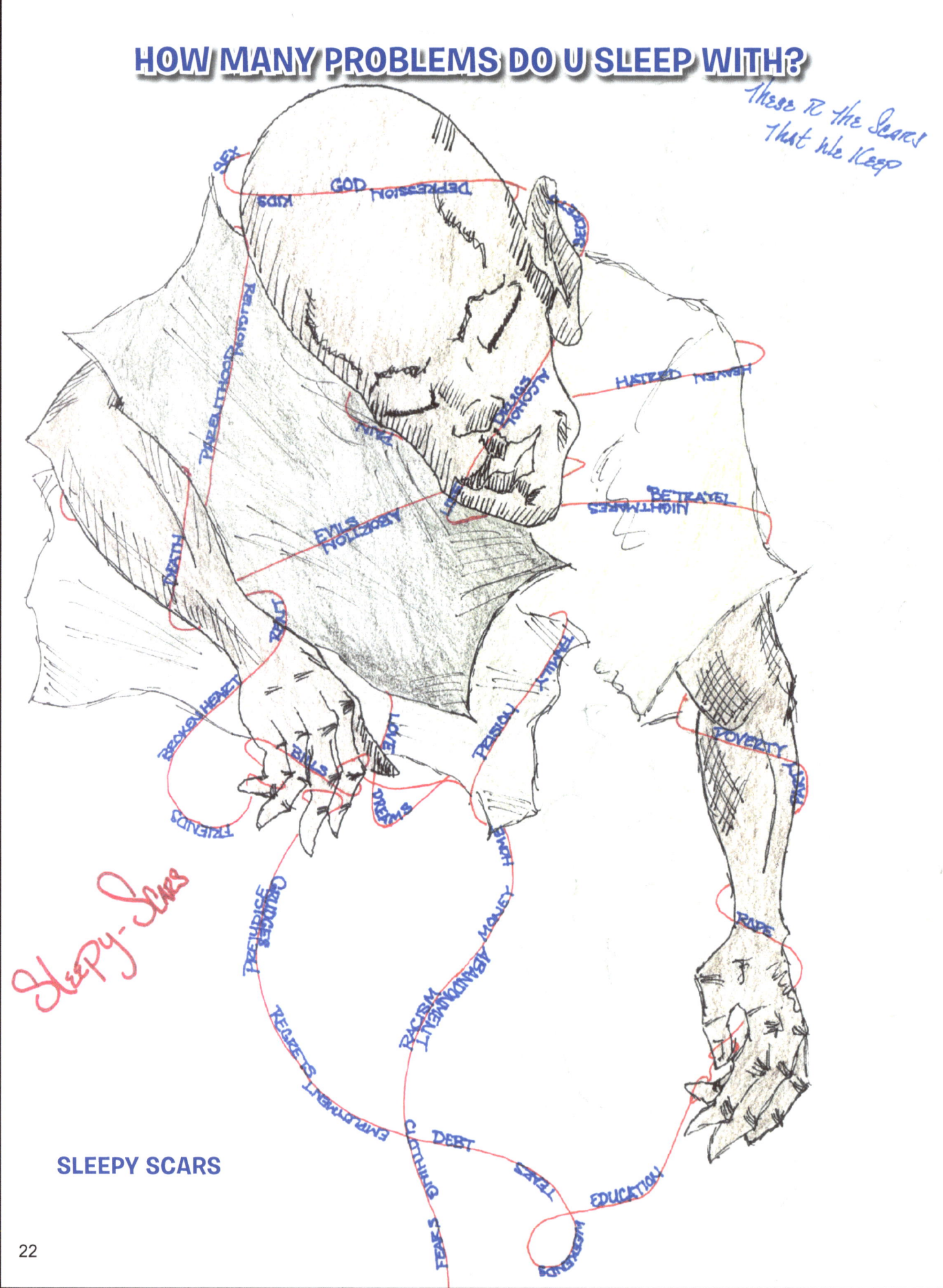

SLEEPY SCARS